Australian Poems

Somewhere in the Sea

By

Tony Woodward

With love

Tony Woodward

Eloquent Books

Eloquent Books
An imprint of Strategic Book Group
P.O. Box 333
Durham CT 06422
www.StrategicBookGroup.com

ISBN: 978-1-60911-948-5

INTRODUCTION

These poems are from a lifetime of thoughts, experiences and feelings. As the title suggests, the sea is a major force behind many of the poems. However, it should be noted that 'the sea' is also a metaphor, not only for the 'sea of humanity', but also the various states of mind I have found myself within whilst writing these poems. I hope you enjoy reading my words and if you are interested in the experiences and stories that lie behind these poems, you can contact me at the following email address:

tonyyoghurt@hotmail.com

This book is dedicated to my late wife, Bev.

In creating this anthology, I would like to acknowledge every human being who has ever loved another.

Table of Contents

Chaos Theory

Full fathom five
My life-blood
The sea
In chaos as in calm
I breathe the blue ansd salty surge
And colours from the corals grow
While paintings run ferocious in my veins
Until they spill liquid-free
I breathe 98% this airy sea

Slaughter (Heaven and Earth)

(Earth)
Fast approaching,
a shore, where feet land unwetted.
Called within all luxuriant minds,
some soft sea smell on shore adrift.
Shouted 'Adventurer' over their heads.
Whispered 'Mutiny' beneath their breaths.

But sand stuck to those quaint shoes,
thrown skeletal beached.
Words from jungle-matted hair,
jungle onomatopoeia.

Fast approaching,
the spear of all deep meanings vetted.
Spasmed kisses came unstuck,
as they stole away from Buda Bridge.
And whispered 'Improper' in tortured mists.
And screamed 'Forever' through parting froth.

But keen the twist of fumes from lips,
run me through so sure.
Love alone so sorely missed,
if deserts be the water's cure.

(Heaven)
We lingered tongues on velvet skin,
perfumed reason with hopes desired.
The murdered images cut so fine,
lay slimed on a river's weeded side.

Standing Children

Where are you going
through numberless streets,
making shadows
with your puppeting fingers
etching at the wall?
So there I catch a broken lip
left open for a message or two.

Back to my garden on this high coast
come the koel in two-toned blue.
And clouds shadowing too, our bodies close,
as if this song had been written for you.

Bamboo Hill

Woken by tremors
after the fugitive was let rest,
I could've untied the dinghy
if I'd been younger, or more indolent.
But, passing fallen heads of rice
lain heavy by the dew,
I knew by those men,
they'd be sliced and dried
in but a few tanned weeks.

His long hair
as he looked up from the tracks,
loosened,
letting the day in front of him,
while white birds dotted the jammy fields,
each leaving others to their own worlds.

(In autumn,
woven tractor pattern space
inside typhoon Number 9
beguiled).

He believes like lions.
He takes the food.
He guards with tense teeth.
As a human,
he is bound to greed.
Yet like a bear in some Hokkaido fog,
he covets the loins of Caravaggio,
while the Buddha is but a stone's throw.

Tony Woodward

Shepherded rocks at dawn

Shepherded rocks at dawn
Above Careel calm
Mirrors
And mirrors
Of it pasted
Like hand-spun welds
And when the bones
Bleached dog-licked
Come humbled
To their Avalon'd skin
The laundered breath
A face
Of smiles
And sin
Below
Evening coming in

A dawn of chattering in the air

A dawn of chattering in the air,
birds easily migrating signs.
Each and every call a scream,
in the caterpillar's hair.

Or deadly earnest windward stealth,
directly fluffed antennae sting.
Locusts swarming garden fed,
princely sheen - a fountain's wealth.

Swallows shiver in static gleam,
feeding from a softer drought.
My sparrows for crows in blackout shed
God here giveth our bluest dream.

Tony Woodward

After Waking   (an unfinished poem)

I wake,
for the rain is falling too fast.
I swear,
moving the tin under the dripping eve.
Movement too, of the headland,
thick with age and perfect mists,
Here upon a pillow that has not worked
since my arrival,
I lie still, sorting the dark from the light,
eyes entranced by visions of the lone hag
with rocks for money.

The room lights up
like a midnight brothel on Bourke.
Yet the dimmer vision of shoji
lay just discernible in a lead-light past.
I have her here beside me,
warm,
with that feint scent of Knowing.
Eyes will now not open gracefully
as the false dawn draws on and on.

Sleep steals back my life,
and I dream…
Wet olives to be my faith, my memory.
A discarding of the French-door look,
and the flood of despair
that was the morning,
runs over the asphalt and into the drain.
I celebrate its

The sculptor without a story…

Air brushes his ears, and somewhat mysteriously loosens the
oily tassels-
wet, raffia-streaked, and darker here and there without curl.
Yet not from the West *this* youth;
Rather, he sways from the Middle East.
It is not day, nor is it evening.
What we do know is that there will be another moon
before the birth of his second child.
This lad, unknown to the earth's foe,
lays footprints facing west,
while on and on the breeze blows-
his torso casting shadows across love's future plains of sadness.
But in his shadow, will a flood of tears lighten such a burden,
when the real joy,
he knows,
is in the last deep breath?

The night before,
as dark memories of colourless acts came thronging in,
a passionate kiss covered cheek,
then cheek.
Boasting poisoned lips
the dew-like sheen,
perverse in all its manner,
sought to dim his smile.
And like pearls around a crown,
white sheets met the dusk-
desert teeth in desert smiles.

The brothers he has met
and kindled with a water-spark,
are lost now, it seems.
But when again this craving to shy away
suffices as reason,
the flesh and blood of the Holy War
will rend his biding lust.
And a hand out-held,
as distant stars redeem
what duly will preside,
shall balance all that blackened gravity will not.
Now centred on such nimble withered limbs,
he wanders quiet-
a follower of the wind.
Told in dreams,
or clouds arranged,
this tale shall never find its mark,
but only live in naked truth
of his features all aflame.
And like a story shed from lip to lip,
undressing days,
and throwing back the pictures
that once amused his soul,
he set to sea,
gouged by a sculptor's will.

I send this card.

I send this card
-a purple heart-
if only to convey my thoughts in colour.
Winds have stained the surface,
like a casual lover's breath.
But who would glisten as shattered glass,
on the morning of the Sabbath?

Attempts have been made:
light (though poor)
eyes
even thoughts
winding
down.

A deserted lane opens into an avenue of yellow leaves.
But you know you are not stable enough
to walk the pathway towards reality
for more than a dream might last.

Love and regards,
Cerulean Blue

Tacsum Café Okayama

I

Coming to the end of the dirt track and fearing the bush in front of me, I notice the pages wrinkle, as if old and full of complaints. The power of vision, even though drawn from the well of smoky-black nights, always tends to leave its jaguar prints upon the page. Claw-scratched scrawl, softened by a smudged sauntering between the lines, leaves nothing but a life in scribble.

II

First bought, the jumper would promise trend, as well as some permanent kind of cliché. Its secrets though, would soon begin to knot and gather, folding along a cable line, or simply wrapping up a naked form. But as the years draped themselves on rusted nails, or crept past icy window jowls, the jumper found its self softened at last, deep between a withering soul's knees to enter the crystals of a dream.

III

Yet truth be known, the weight of loneliness lay instead, carving, slicing and scraping deeper into the marrow, before his closing inner eye. How thickly it threatened - the nectar that could so easily, so rapidly, form the miracle that is forgiveness. Those who have been loved, with teeth touching flicking tongue, are often left parched out on the wires of salivaless boundaries. Metals forge in knitted embrace, loins writhe and tremble and out come the monsters, dancing with god-breath - as if I should have known. As if I should have learned by now - the forbidden paths of the jaguar.

Horse

I have not dwelt in shadows
(shadows cast but short memory).
If I love the chase,
If I close my eyes,
All around is light,
And desire no disgrace.

Through the glass of night
A friend arrives,
Refracted and clear,
Pounding so hard on my heart.
It is as if he has broken all my skins,
And masks alike.
And still he beats at my heart
In perfect rhythm,
With a pulse such
That I know not who is he.

Hc (with a capital)

Jesus
my boyhood friend
my boyfriend in the glass
voice lover
fever giver

voice as strong as you want beneath the fear
when we lived under sheets
trapping song and intoxicating hymns
words that became the Light in darkness
dress'd in wings and soft-cheek colours
Jesus

Gone
the myth
a prop
an experiment that blew up
leaving severe scarring
beyond recognition they tell me
and who would recognise me now
the goodness gone in a fit of anger
that has lasted twenty five years
if He was betrayed once
then He betrays me a dozen times a day
I mark off each neglected disciple
and de-pray

Even then
was it cheaper by the dozen
Jesus

Coat-hanger Blues #16

At thirty two, the smallest feathers floating by.
Dunhill behind the ears and
tartan cloak enclosed
water crescents,
strung from mud lawns.

Smile all day,
Any day.
No, not…
never bored.
Not at all in Buddah's dream.

But the time within us all is not enough.
No time, but for the lotus.
Symbols on those soft petals
pasted with calm,
strung from mud lawns.

I cannot find when.
I need not suffer pain.
I need not be.

Swapped the white blossoms for stern rocks,
fever mountain kneaded.
Then a neck so daintily drawn-in,
complains softly in this gallery
the works,
strung from mud lawns.

Running, you are soon swamped.
Bugger it!
Bugger youse all.

So you manage your mirrors at cost.
And idling at every pose
you are hung up in coat-hanger blues,
strung from mud lawns.

Stained (There was no other way to reach the water than to walk)

The creek.
There afloat,
breathing shallow in shallow waters,
my love waits with watery lungs,
almost hidden
in creek reeds.

The bank,
where you find the animal tunnels sculpted,
woven through with grass and twig,
and crawl
where lantana towers.

Would you have lived beyond the flood
if I had promoted your creek-smile?
The blood on your cheek stirs
under another watery tear.
My Ophelia by far.

every now and then I find myself in prayer

expanse of ochre-yellow light
left in shadow.
one man scratched his ear and strode off naked over sandy
concrete
the sun becomes wind against the body
the body I will soon lose
as women suck on their men
as I suck on my pipe - the one with ancient designs
though my nipples quiver too
I neglect the sex
and swallow in the waves of heat

every now and then I find myself in prayer
a prayer for the poor as Lisarow oranges rot
a prayer for you bound in old skins
somewhere in Tokyo
then again a prayer for us all
inside the universal sarcophagus
and those bloody prayer wheels chattering as they fly overhead
round and round from Tibet to Tibet
forever

now the decadence warrants warm forbidden faith
then the unprotected sex
blood and sperm spill across the sallow chests of the dead
during the expected storms of murder
though the faith that patterned my torso's flesh under archaic chants
reaches no further than my own body

I become Pietro from Varese
green olive branches hang from my shoulders
the head of white flowerless marble smiles its own love away
it starts to decay
but all too slowly

yet we have time to wait
another torso is hewn from the virgin snow
only the neck lacerated red

next time you're here
I want to drink poppy juice with you
until both our foreheads hit the kotatsu
onegaishimasu

Tony Woodward

Waiting for a southerly

I

He looks worried, worrying kindness away.
What about the gardener? Busy brown,
and the tag.
I'm worried because Gwen rang from the green phone.
I'm worried because Gwen is down and out in Tempe.
I'm worried I sell too many eggs, on the whole.

Across the globe
bit by bit less fluent,
by bits.
And not wanting grace to show.

I am not worried at all now.
My knee is twitching, and sometimes I can feel
my memory pulses.
Wave after wave pushing on the rocks.
Peninsula brackets,
waiting for the southerly buster.

I will pretend seasickness -
Christened.
To float across sandy sea-beds
(misty sand and coral lace
gone too soon the swirling face)

II

The crossing: ESCALATION OF VIVISECTION.
We feared being found amidst the sandstone,
the oysters,
the spotted octopii,
the sea-horses,
without a message.

When you find someone else's bones,
that's when,
when the southerly comes.

Coming to life

Whimper at the losses incurred.
Count the strands of straw along the tatami.
Switch the saliva from one side to the other.
And pause.

To see death just sitting there, moaning too...
It was the night when he might have crushed my chest;
when I was alive with it;
swimming in the mess of love.
When my heart was all over my flesh
and I felt ugly and raw.
When you think your breath will stop at each
STRANGLE HOLD.
But there,
your limbs bind
and he IS your only means of survival.

If you could see my hands,
as still as death.
The tablets gone.
The steel still held tight in the fingers.
My head resting heavily on my right arm.
I feel the bone as my skull presses away the arm's flesh.
A tear rolls out of the left eye,
across the bridge,
and down into my right eye.
It finally falls onto my jumper's warmth at its sleeve.
Now,
as I come to life,
I see the glistening marks at the wrist.

The Well

From the bottom of the well
it is hard to see who peers down.
Yet you have no qualms
about offering some reflection
of that tattered light.

If we could mark the soul
at certain points along our lives,
to notice where the scars are redder.
Or even lift the lids of flamboyance
beneath which Doric proportions cry,
then we have dared.
Simple fate built on excess pain
truants in swathes of mortality.

(The voice, alerting one to the earlier presence of the hundred
dolphins,
had not near finished with what had been missed, if not lost.
On it went, in ides of anger and astonishment-
though of course ceding that the irate male
was perfectly within his rights)

Why *this* question?

the heart is wretched
torn like seaweed
from the caressing fathoms
dying up on sea gulled sands
salt-scented
for what man has done to man
can never be erased
or nullified with pardon

the rotten faces
smeared with anger
or perchance relief
caking in the sun
and I in sleepless torment
perpetuate the grudge

vile hatred
has bitten deep
I spit on greed
I curse your lies in faith
yet still unconscious
I rob sleep
passing time with a stronger pain killer

tonight
the soul is lost
depression
coiling vilification and deception
are what's on offer
though more than you deserve

I spit on your dead face
as huge bats cloister above

Tony Woodward

Deciding to stay at home for Australia Day

The floor was covered with eiderdown,
sheets, and blankets.
There,
he waited for the night to drop its noise.
Was smothered,
humid.
And in the dawn
the calm would smother it all.

Waking up,
breathing out,
especially the BAD,
wondering if you had liked it.

Listening to you
speaking English
English langwich
loving you,
my secret pink-nearly-blue.
I am bound to show myself
a little too much.

Vegemite as taste;
or oily-thick on canvas.
And drops of wheat on a sheaf
I'd planted in the garden late spring,
harvested now,
ripe,
the head resting on your cheek.

And at first light,
the calm will smother us both.

Petchaburi

The floor boards had been worn smooth
like vast summer tans.
He pushed his hand across at least a foot of wood
before he reached a crevice.
If you crouched and looked through,
you could see cows moving,
pissing long sounds.
And soon the stench of rising humidity.
The sarong tightens with the exaggerated spying,
and there, in that veil of eyes-closed-black,
was the thought of tearing cotton.

The light suddenly went out;
his mother having her own way
or just to hide us all
from the shame of distance in the night.
Just as suddenly,
came his hand on my arm.
Had I my prayer mat?

A night with C (from boys to men)

Thinking I had it all,
I found Elizabeth and English Entrance Failure.
But that was only the start.

Jealousy, juxtaposition and
all manner of judgment prevailed.
From Skye Ceremonies
to Kneeling Before the Third Kaiser.
In disbelief I swore at the employee
who closed in on my centre of gallantry,
as if he had had a brain to go with *that* heart.

They hang on to each other
as I hang from a far thinner rope.
In knowledge we make for the bridge,
by-passing tracks in our glitzy night clothing.

Sydney Central city cinema
complex sex.
They have planted wooden boxes with pansies.
But real people tend to board buses
within their own messed up mania.
And he sings 'I'll grab you when we get there'.
So, like Uriah Heep and organ mists,
we drift ultimately intimate.

Greek taxi driver opens his loins.
as if clothes could be burnt so easily by lust.
But it was too late for ceremony;
too late for caring.

And the lips of man
and the reasons of existence
and those suffering so far from Athena,
cause one to reflect in time,
from boys to men.

What was it you said?

What was it you said?
'Drive the nail'?
My fingers are raw, dad.
Dad!

In your camouflaged plane high above the ripened ridges…
dreaming
Were you at this height?
Or just 'In charge'?
I am happy you only dropped supplies dad,
and not bombs
that would have surely
crippled and killed unknown-
and then the choking
from melted metal.

Anyway,
what did you say, dad?
You drove and drove across the Territory,
looking for a track out?

Depression on Wednesday 24th March 2004

Aim for green, I thought…
depression needs a tranquil grave.

As I walked, I thought of wasted years.
Although filled with experiences,
or even moments of joy,
it is now, of course, that they are all forgotten.

I headed for the tennis courts.
A youth was walking across the oval.
(I keep my eye on him,
and the lady-postie seated outside the change sheds)
If I'd had my camera
I would have shot them both.
And maybe some fuzzy blow-ups later.

She had offered me the paper.
An offer I declined.
I just wanted to read my book.

After the voice had cracked the isolation,
I lay down on the bench,
taking off my shoes.
I placed one beneath my head and
the other beneath me, rather too neatly,
on the grass
in a soft-leather manner.

As I held my novel on outstretched arm
suddenly a siren stuck up into the air.
At the same time a woman's voice from the courts
rose in such similar tones
that I thought she was mimicking the ambulance
(or whatever it had been).

The thing about lying on a bench
is that you can see
the sky as one hugeness.
Today, seven pelicans floated across
in an arrow formation,
and directly above me
broke into what was more like
a slow ballet movement;
swirling in eights and infinities
to then regroup and soar away
as a slow moving V.
Over three hours of pacing through a memory
in some delinquent-like hatred.
Time marries.
And without honeymoon you are glued
to long, slouching minutes,
touched by views of suburbia-
its old men dressed as old WWII gents,
ambling along concrete footpaths
towards very private plans.

I loosen up towards noon,
balanced between my birth and my death,
yet still unwilling to show any happiness,
even though it is my darling dead mum's birthday.

Going back to the visions
of library fed ART, it is
NOT what lures me.
NOT at all perceptive, NOT inspiring, NOR awesomely
painted.
NOTHING that would save me from
the overdose dream.
I rise. I go.
Across the hidden greens of Erina's vomit.

Where do you wake this stricken morn
(a song)

Where do you wake this stricken morn,
all marble slow-eyed gaze?
A ceiling in Chippendale,
too smashed to return?
Or Maroubra-sheets to your groin?

Chorus:
Suffer to love, suffer to leave,
kisses 'neath the brine.
Suffer to love, suffer to leave,
Futures oft' entwine.

Southern Rights pass you by,
a dawn of gold and blue.
Their song to your ear, sad mermaids adrift,
their gills an outlandish cry.

So wreck me on your crystal chest,
or find that coral shore,
that blood won't colour so deep a hue,
a crucifix Benedict blessed.

I search beneath your eyelid smile,
chaos theorems caught.
But what is love but this raw mime,
that holds us here awhile?

Tony Woodward

Maisie's Question

An ovation of sorts
as locusts purrr
across smart lands
tethered to life
by tractor
and train

'interferin' with our lives. Bastards!'
Maisie blurts hot-headed
over tea and sad timtams
powdered
or cloud-soft pastel cheeks
matched to the colour of the swarm
hovercrafting now over a landscape
that has lost its tune

'fuckin' hell!'
Maisie wails
surreptitious disappearance
of leaf and limb
they gaze
lickin' their chops
in a delicate haze

there's no raffle here
in this totalitarian regime
this season's grace
comes to turn your gut
just when you wanted to die anyway
Maisie sighs

'Where are you when I need you Roy?'
And purrrs
'Roy Boy?'

Tony Woodward

Come to the Continent

bring me your bile
your wolverine smile
the churches are open
in Europe tonight

Sorrow Ocean

Now, have I suddenly lost you after too short a time together?
I sit on this sunny Glebe doorstep,
almost to tears.
My own body yours,
and my nervous reaction to the hands
that had trembled on my lap,
now ceaseless.

You leave me alone
drying my Victoria Park swimming pool wet hair on this March
doorway.
I was so captivated?
God, these tears should fall plainly after
so many.
So many.
Yet, they remain as complicated as the rest
as they dribble into Sorrow Ocean.

My eyes squint.
I cannot see tomorrow.
I cannot see the Lord.
Dormant time,
as cars, as death, moves around me.
Even I have that longing to be loved.
Yet there is no love on this street.
It is always behind something;
hidden in bedrooms,
or spilt onto carpeted floors.
You cannot expect love in a Sydney car
from one whose disguise has been painstakingly moulded

over so many years.

Now, I want you.
I want to lie in a quiet room of love,
with only your scattered fingers searching my secret
movements.

I find a cigarette butt in the gutter,
pick it up,
then throw it down again.
Our bodies, though not so light,
seemed to have been just as carelessly handled.
The endless children...
their footsteps so Australian on these old footpaths.
I am not dreaming of these concrete squares,
where we all pray that our initials shall lie
scratched forever.
(I am not dreaming).
Now, I am not smiling in anger at you.
This voicelessness is just a deeper vow.
How does one forgive Allah's repulsion of the boy-boy?
I blame neither myself,
these prancing leaves, nor the dead youth in his smallish coffin.
(I am not smiling)

If I had that magic ring,
I would slip it on my finger
to ward off those future lovers
that line up for miles,
sharpening their knives.

I am guilty of exposure to the sun.
I am guilty of presence of mind.

But I am not guilty of the future murders
that will be committed under the name of this skin;
under my name.
All presiding judges know this.

Leaves,
and children,
still dance down this concrete footpath.

Captive

Child at a window
fingering at long perspirations
her green-faced eyes
Arabic hewn history
his toy
his scene
history

So she shifts her anklet of gold
to swerve around
another fear
another night
another bold tear falls

Emblazoned
I say EMBLAZONED
Redfern-iron-shed-hid
tied her hands and hoped
for the grace of Allah
to permit

Spots of the Leopard

· You dread the thought of my coming back
posing as the sinner.
Or at least
finding your pillow for you.
After we had eaten the last of each other's breaths,
it wasn't long before the leopard came in,
tail stroking my thigh,
as in the quiet nightmare.

It was in that dream
how the eyes crossed,
then turned inside,
watching for what you had to offer.
And looking down,
my thigh burned as if stung.
You spied me through those vegan eyes,
praying,
like a mantis within reach of its furry moth.

Sliding down your speckled pelt,
and without flinching,
I watched
as you devoured me in a bloody orgy
under the odour of snow.

Tony Woodward

The Silent S

almost touching my foot
the earth surrounds
so fertile
holding the proud mushroom head
with more oil in the ochre
or RED on its edge

no
I will not BLEED
by your eyes forever
or forever and ever

forever inside my foul wounds
you lick and lick and lick
in places whipped
by sun-faded lashes

they
the precious
will feign blindness
where light enters and grows

and so
we meet once again
you don't talk
and I don't forget
in that fibro house
near Cape Hawke

amen

Do not consider remembering the forget-me-not fragrance

Do not consider remembering the forget-me-not fragrance
of wild, wild paspalem-soaked silver arvos
and green
sun-covered envy from a door ajar.

A slut, a whore;
the journeyman's longing
inside this lazy light's night
before the flight of man.

Yes,
into this night's dreams,
a love!
But hope of love forlorn-
this gangster seed on a sock of mine.

Somewhere in the Sea

Secrets
stilled in silted minds,
throw a line out
beyond the sand,
and dismiss them whiting
as they butt at their grainy bed.
In the deeply painted weed
come the leatherjacket,
to suck in rot and rhythm.
And blowing dust clouds
among the dirtier remnants of green,
disappear intoxicated.

As luck would throw
drunk light to lace the deep,
seeps to its death
where sea-boy fossils grow.
Had once hard arms and mainsail pluck,
steel to steel asleep.

Oh light!
Lift night to the crystal chinking,
while shape and sound dry saline beads
upon bare-breasted youth.
And with this salted age
they stride through dreams
that love might come,
wintering into spring.

Peter's Café Wyong

To step inside you, the other world,
across glass,
those huge, white teeth would be mine;
only discernable in mirrors.
Or the rose windows of the 8:20,
waving,
and waving your child's arm too,
crooning from Fassifern
into wattle-woven shade.

'A fork each?'
She can smile!
And they share a carrot cake
this side of a wide blue sky.
And almost-cream chimneystacks
melting pre-dawn passengers
for Town.

I have my bill.
And I shall
always remember
being there,
inside Peter's Café.

Poorman's Bay

A norwester blows the crap
from Castle Cove into my tiny poorman's bay.
I get the free things:
plastic and cans and
oysters full of meat and metal.
The lot!

A dirty day is this
that runs itself through my hair.
Man and dog meander across the rocks
with discordant dodges.
The pressure is painfully obvious-
eyes as windows
checking my empty bonds,
willing my poverty to eat into the bone.

They once frolicked here
-he with the solidly unstable eyes
-she with her mouth to his gaze.

A fish jumps from the olive brown;
feels the wind for that second in time
and decides against the growth of wings;
the pee-wee world.

The mind-set of this haunt sickens.
As betrothed as white weddings to
their new extensions,
their new render,
their new bark,

they are.

It is all I can do
to stop myself feeding on these clinging shellfish
slicing the lips as a globule of snot-like flesh
slides in with the clotting blood.
Those that hover above the tide
burn under the sun,
baking slowly,
forging their stock of heavy metals
into idol design.

They found him on his back,
legs dribbling down the old sandstone-block wall,
heels whimpering above the 'pop-pop' of drying oyster edges,
pen now floating between his fingers,
eyes that hoped for a revival slightly ajar.
It was not death-
just a plastic nap.

the final word (after the tsunami)

why do ye not understand my speech
is it without compassion
without rhyme

with them they have brought in the sunny days
alongside the chariots of fire
indeed given peace
where peace is due
alas
shown signs too
of prophetic doom
yet still
we walk into the tide
into the waves of God's love
washing our wills away
into infinity

these days he writes his own obituaries
élan-lapsed
in true consultation
and on pure white parchment
he is judged by HE who is the ONLY ONE

a soul shivers
knowing who be next
to disrupt the water's calm
'whither I go, ye cannot follow'
he whispers

his final word

This night my daughters

This night finds its silence
now.
Now that the roses have been left
in a friend's loving hands.

Ah, but the scent lingers…
In words.
In smiles.
That unsaid happiness of daughters.

If I am strong at this moment,
it is due to an abandonment of fear.
For I know
that if I was to ever fall,
they would give their eyes so strong
to secure my soul,
woven tight
in a net
of such soft, loving tones.

To Bev

In between classes
I catch my breath.
One knows that overhead there is love-
that element always so high above life.
Just to ponder the altitude
leaves me small and skyless.

I have left my home
and come to these warm, pathetic tatami,
the smell of which
promises to overwhelm-
to *ab-so-lutely* cover my brutal soul.
A warm, brown, grass-dead hue
to breathe,
to paint my ribs-
even in their valleys.

When she turned round
I was not following her every movement,
so her back came as a simple surprise-
naked then, under the sun.
And those well-known shoulders,
limp in love with the summer.

Then, before I knew it,
she had entered the sea
as even part of me.
But I had gone.

And she, living on there-
on the beach,
watched the headlands to the south
receding in their slow haze.

Tony Woodward

the eyes that all men use (for Yukio)

those men
superb in their blank nudity
running delirious in the snow
somehow manage
to dismantle their *mikoshi* right under my gaze
eyes flashing
focusing
and their fireworks belting out the gunpowder pulse

across the bay
a perfect wind rushes towards death
while grey-white sleek stripes
slip their way down mountain ridges
and fade

the lake
in tune
swells with gusting blasts
and throws the children's voices into caverns deep
to sleep
there
until the swellings of their adolescence stir

the youth
driven back and back
as the teeth are sucked at by each wave of wind
dreams of the sensual blood plunge
and dives into that coated flesh
red on blue

then finally
one so close
whose lips chatter as if real
all his eyelids I close
so as to swim inside that very
black scene

over there
on the three islands
there is no gnashing of teeth for Manu

Jesus' Sperm

Born in the Philippines to the religion of fervour,
you often regret being named Jesus.
At the height of circumcision,
you also regretted its paucity.
'Jesus' -like it's just part of the menu.
Then you spot yourself in the nave,
in other moulds,
as glass,
or under glaze.
Or even on the cross,
wretched, hovering,
reaching with both hands to claim a softer pseudonym,
you smoke your own rising blood.

Once you go down the ladder,
into the wet-dream cave,
you know the score.
Facing the waves,
the uncle speaks in tongues.
(the voice of spume beyond,
acrimonious,
yet pledging your salvation above *Tito*'s blithering)
Then he comes at you,
face a'twitch, clenched fist steady

We know it is Saturday, and Jesus is about.
His rib cage bleeds somewhere in Manila.
I have counted 17 times
(and lost count too).
He calls it purification - I *shall* be purified.

So I lay my trunks down on the salty cave-dirt,
and the humbling humidity is pleased.
Tito is exultant-looking
(even handsome-looking, with his tanned skin and blackheads)
as I come, dripping down onto the cave dust.

Discriminating is what I do.
I see the differences all too easily
as they covet their roles of peculiarity.
But from the shadows of our cave
I see the sameness-
and the same resurrection
out to sea.

Deserting Cities of the Heart

On the road side,
when all was said, or being said,
your eyes grew light with swelling tears,
and your beauty was unbounded.
Focused photos will often cloud the moment in mist,
but your perfection will always mist my fucking eternal logic.
YOU breathe the air I breathe,
YOU see the light I see,
your body hurts, as does mine,
and so in sweat and passion we bide.

There is no need for my surrender-
for who, or what, would I surrender to?
With each step taken towards your sage-said fate,
I consume, as a sky consumes its planet.
And I just eat and eat YOU.

The seas may rage,
and storms, alighting from their tempest,
might scream their adoration.
But within the sanctity of our pure mortality,
I have decently ripped open every vein
for YOU.
I have tossed my heart towards
horizons unknown
for YOU.
I have swum within your breath,
as any molecule must.
If there needs be a god,
then I have YOU.

In this ugly landscape along this road,
your presence withers all that surrounds YOU.
Your burning beauty sears,
as if under God's deep wrath.
Yet apparent annihilation
is replaced by radiant light.
I dream
I will touch your very soul one day.
I dream
I will dream
one night
of YOU.

Fucked-Up Body-Bomber

The Divine:
A uniform of white, a sky of London blue,
and written in sinc to rapped-out lines of the Koran.
(you can't guess where we are now, can you?)
But still,
this felicity intrudes like a smile after confession.
Morphic wings, grown from the bone,
begin to cast their breadth upon the wind.
After a glance, we fly above Trafalgar's
tousled feathers,
shouldered by your strength and beauty.
Now, lift me up
and up,
into the angels' realm,
as bound to another as one could ever be.

The Poem:
Stagnant licence plays below,
a slow and wanton tune.
As eyes one caught in some sun's light,
your body I stroked 'til blue.
Let those who say paradise is near,
beg to wonder still.
For here is mine - a future clear,
programmed for the kill.

The Shining Path

Returning from the beach
where gold was gold
and eyes sat in years of ag*ed* stone,
you said things that I now forget
and things that you didn't say
I still remember.

I took you into my sad loving arms,
where you forgave
and the truth I braved.
How I could have taken the rivers away
on whatever I chose as jetsam,
buoyed by that wide grey sea.
How I could have buried your tears
as the dunes rolled beneath my thunder.

But still, I attacked your innocence
until I could no longer be myself.
Then retraced each sandy footprint
with abandoned curiosity,
back along the shining path.

To Love You

The sore night,
bleeding mists and unseen voices.
Occasional movement screams upon the moist air
in a dirty olive smear.
Behind the willow strands
(where he uses dirty lubricant
-those foreign oils sticky to the fingers)
he sits alone in his housing estate.

Criss-cross reflections of silken-set bronze
first polished yesterday, glow.
The nude, struck over and over,
like the kissed Christ-feet in Catholic countries.
Or that Thai wat in the soft sun,
melting the weld.

We find our way
into the souls of others;
our pumice fumes
breathing into each other's hours.
Forgetting about everything,
the tight cotton weave
willows over the contours of our loins.

To love you,
perfumed and quiet.
You talking,
holding cashews in your palm.
To love you.
And I forget about anything.

Pyre

The fear,
as fire fingers in casual rape.
It's North Head alight,
while steel-blue harbour cowers
and the sweet browns from palettes spew
across sail and pacific sea.
Little orange flames poke,
while my daddy cries from the sky
near
his bloody belov*ed* gully.

Retaliation,
and the stomach, offering its muscles stroked smooth
-a reddened agenda
-a forgiveness plea.
My god, in a feverish backward step, retires,
as if cursed by the reflection
of that simple dose of flame.

You want to perve into your ancestor's lives,
forward marching
on those training days,
when Jack, not yet the father,
held that solid air
in lungs of steel,
his mates in pieces posted home
from the morose office in Darwin.

And if he were held so,
by rope or whatnot,
to his manly northern cliff,
then I as much,
hang
by
that
same
sense
of
string
above the stealth of the pyre,
eyes blurred,
from this female ferry.

Too many Catholics in Naples

Flesh forward, and pouring the unnumbered
in a small child's world,
the eyes are in the immediate
-in the no-vice situation.
Now, eternally grateful for those puberty years,
of jeans tightening
and ragged-torn.
It seems the spaces are either limitless
(when she was around)
or confined;
over within the hour.
'Time should be measured by love' I said,
sucking in the concrete fields of Bondi.

Neapolitan purse snatchers:
possibly the capitalists she had thought irrelevant.
'Communism will lead Italy out' she said.
'Could you bear all those burning crosses?' I persisted,
without meaning to put it directly onto Jesus.
'There are just too many Catholics in Naples.
But still, you have a view over the bay.'
(where Francesco had taken off his shirt
up the front of the boat
and wondered whether to dive into that azure glass.
Or not)

If love passed us by,
it was not because we did not realise we were in love,
but rather,
that both the waters off Capri,

and the swell of Bondi breakers,
could only reflect our own disabilities.
We are but effigies in our own tiny niches-
the fruit of history's vast loins.

You climb to Lennon's 'yes'
to find love is just the poison
taking effect.

You went past Woy Woy

You are square below your eyes-
below Spain even.
Nodding alongside your 'blue period' queen,
and shouldered by her face of clay,
you are a boy-
a bronze medallion.
Did you meet in Alexandria?
Or perhaps on the docks at Chios?
Your swarthiness teems
into my eyes
when your head nods back.
And the train caresses.
But there!
Like an architecture of the flesh,
lies your Corinthian neck.

A man now,
from Thessaloniki
(and once even ferried to Palermo).
Alas, these ancient cities are not ours to rebuild.
But you are of *all* towns to me.
You are the Fassifern night,
and the Hamilton mosaics.
You are both the divine cause,
and the effect.
And thus it is
that these small towns rejoice.
You wake and rub an eye, then stretch;
as if muscle were your every move.

As you both depart Woy Woy
in the wedded bliss of youth,
a line of light left over
from the Hawkesbury night,
streams into your futures.
And from the platform of love
I sing softly to myself,
'On and on, as a European sky,
in foggy pane delights the eye.
Then on and on, as caged birds fly,
you threw me too soon that delinquent sigh'.

Preservation

Stinging syringes seed purple loam
Beneath a perforated sky
Jelly-roll monsters out
Blushing humiliation
The sour-sweet blues from Mick's guitar
Gutters our conversation
While bones are given their lots
In paralysed graves so poorly dug
And we are shelved there
We are kept in air
As bloodied brains
Or hearts of rye

Seldom woven with ripening seams
Your veins lay blood-stuck beneath my scars
And your gold given in gamble
Whilst some noise
In this criss-cross neon night
Fixated with your hollow ears
Slowly digs in

As steel falls into plastic domes
You take harvest of the past
Without a thought
For your empty hessian bag
Bleeding with a ton of new memories

Tony Woodward

M.R. The Man from Merimbula

Night elopes with nothing new,
yet comes a'running for his bride.
Down the track of banksia bends,
onto the beach without a tide.

With willow hands 'neath moonlight balm,
and stepping out with porpoise grin,
waves of dawn far out to sea,
lap naked on his soul within.

He crouches down where waters kiss,
to feel the warmth of an ocean's sand.
Locked still inside the waves' wet dream,
slow fingers crawl upon the land.

Across the pastel red and green,
he writes his mariner's oath anew.
Fingers painting creeping free,
the night's away on spinifex dew.

He waits for dawn; for footprints foxed,
at Browlee Heads for calm to land.
While naked Baba deflowers the strand,
the seaweed sings of Merimbula Man.

Beside the dawn

Beside the dawn
you barge in unannounced,
with seagull shit on your shoulder;
like you've come up all sad and sore
without a periscope or something.
Your fallen rocks
-those gifts glued to the sea-
on each swelling tide,
swallow men in shadow.
Their wires of breath
spin by reel and gleaming string-
Giacometti ornaments at best.
Frail, dribbled sand mounds
from a child's cupped hands
suddenly solidify below the shivering prayered paws.

Oh headland!
Don't *you* quiver so.
Hidden amidst your tors
is but the sedimentary soul
-the sandstone thespian,
who juggles lead sinkers
that would take us blinkered down
through boiling surge
to Neptune's sigh.
And dive as deep as deep could be,
to tail mermen's glinting scales
even to a deeper drone.

Above the dawn,
the sea has set her sperm adrift;
has come undone,
to corrode her liquefied lands.
And a softer rust from musty waves
will sail ashore
to stain the virgin sands anew.

punkpoem

This poem could've been written by a 15 year old,
if he'd had the guts like.
The world was made in 7 days;
just a speck that spun in space
picking up all this stuff.
God made the sea and shit,
and wrapped it round,
like cool moss for the low bits.
He got his man Noah to alight,
along with all these animals...

Fuck! I've forgotten about Adam and Eve,
and that apple and shit.
And he made the light,
and every living, loving thing could see what they were fucking
up to.
Adam withdraws from Eve and buries his head behind that
bloody fig leaf.
As if *he* was the culprit!

Much later,
Cranach did this kind of painting,
and just the colour of their flesh
will tell you how this poem's
going to end…
like pumice and shit.

Morning Walk

A long time wandering through the snow,
then finally a stream
and what appears to be moss,
seeped in such a brilliant green,
set against a glacial icy blue-whiteness.
I have followed
maybe rabbit footprints to this place.
Now, as I proceed down
with the water's cool sound,
birds begin to warn of my presence.
I am of thunderous joy.
I choose to lick my wounds through prayer,
knowing that I have found the colours of life again.
Last night's solid block of murderous sleep
splits under the axe.
Yet the sound is of honest toil.

Man's fate,
defined here on this mountain side,
is on occasion a bitter struggle
within its timely separation from truth.
If only I could consistently reveal the truth-
or what I believe to be the truth.
If I could hold that face again in my hands,
look skilfully into those delicate promises,
and simply remember what to say.
Whether I truly awake before my death
one will never know;
our birth and death lie centuries apart.
But I realize that I have already lost you.

I have lost you in the colours of sound
amongst the millions that have ventured behind my eyes.

Maybe my staring
is the confrontation of who I am.
Could my breathing reveal who I should become?
But these thoughts are just dreams,
led by tears back along my own neglected track.
Should you smile upon my return,
I shall take the hint
and start sifting the sands for a possible motive.
I am the world and the world is yours,
as I say my prayers in the talking in tongues.

Tony Woodward

tablecloth faith is no religion

tablecloth faith and indelible memories
cruise low over Lebanese orchards.
while pa's got the new stove,
still the black table
beckons them all to the feast.
should we pray without a father?
our father who art in heaven..
et. al.
prayer ends.
we rise.
peached cheeks smudged rusted brown in heat
nearly umber
in chiaroscuro movie-show stands
and massive forms of light
distilling into the night
down where they quietly murdered the Norfolk pines

we wear our berets for your gallery visits.
they wear their baseball caps for lust
(those delicious eyes below the brim).
soldiers of the forest
teem in to get drunk on the nectar
from this tadpole jar sitting
always
always
near the laundry tub.
'close the door' she yells...
'w'ya born in a tent?'

Borneo

It was somewhere in the mountains-
a snow-field high and darkened by cloud
and a sticky mist that surrounded our bodies.
There were many people skiing fast,
as if on roller-coasters.
Tracks followed tracks-
almost like a burnt taste,
or maybe just that simple fear inside a butterfly net.

When I awoke, I had forgotten my manners
And left her sleeping
naked as I.

She seemed to live within clear visions
of past perfection;
the pacific ocean touching her toes near the tent.
I wondered then
if she was still in love with her memories.

In Borneo
the radicals of my person swallowed
that thick river - veins to prey upon.
Kept swimming til the Rajang River bank brushed my chest.
Then tried to hold on to the water-plants
that in turn held on to their own mud.
Too fast, those little brown boys called BRAVERY;
braving a surge from a young current.
And holding, holding.
The fuscous river rushed past their dark curves,
like a lover over his lover.

Leonard seeks me out; ties me up
then releases, as if the roots had lost their muddy grip.
I slouch, hiding within my guilt,
and let the waves of seduction
trace their salted seaweed arc upon my beach.
From grey memory
I pattern my palette
with a dusky bloodied swab
from a second world war wound.

Red

A colour-
a sticky liquid set on sullen knives,
when all goes wrong;
with the kids,
with the wife.

Tonight we enter the museum,
wiping our brows on the heavy
stone walls-
almost convict built,
until THAT RED
begins to mar our tans.

And so we presume change,
thinking aloud,
before our mirrors deliver a similar insanity.
'You done the dirty on 'em...
You gotta pay'.
So they slit our throats with their own sullen knives,
right there and then in the midst of
THAT RED.

Tony Woodward

Just a boy

The outbreak of laughter;
outbroken, uncriminal, anti-terrorist
-socialism at its best!
The ticklish perforations
of dormitory darkness,
numbing, nefarious evenings,
when even the close air
appeared naked.
Such pretence
in the unbroken line of pain;
unexpurgated;
solely due to our master's needs.
Binding,
blinding,
till bound to the end;
as if in this place
such pleasure was etched instead
into that bony candle wax.
And muffled soprano screams
(that could never be whispered OUT LOUD)
our only song.

You sit on a wooden bench;
the shimmering depths of jarrah
have put you under another spell.
And you're thinking of 'the wall',
where things had, in those days, just ended up.
Now, the prosecutor,
with his whip and wig,
flogs the air instead,

until your brain bursts with memories
of that 1968 holiday, of sorts.
And his eyes (as 'the prince of darkness')
tend the jungle within.

You juggle the syllables.
You slice what's left into bits you can handle:
re-mi-ni-scence.
You juggle a few words
to remain calm in the sudden downpour of fear.
You wait for the sentence…
It's "GUILTY!" (as always)

Tony Woodward

Plaited Wedding

This day has held a thousand fears,
and memories refuse to find
those idle, rambling creek bed reeds,
enough of black to make a sky.

In love-torn tears a fervent dawn
I rose, forgot to iron again,
and sank into the day forlorn,
surrendering all despondent pain.

Then covered prayers in blackened luck
soot-shadows cast upon the night,
A cleansing brought such anchored thoughts;
my funeral should've had the right.

Tell tales beneath that blackened sky.
Hail truth through such redeeming lies.
And if we die to pass our lies;
hearts defile in abhorrent cries.

As Christ once helped the blind to see
with several days of brilliant signs,
even Ararat seemed so clear
the seven-pointed star maligned.

As sculptures then horizon-lined,
and time to soon submerge and rust.
In chrome a wayward moral quake
shall last in perfect plaited trust.

As Jesus bled, her tears did fall,
ten fingers strayed then did entwine.
Though filigree smiles were hidden behind,
sad veins of antiquated wine.

Revival of the Hedonist

Your putative friend,
through private intention,
prevails long-winded in sermon-speak.
The remains of his parasitic phrases
muscle in on our ears.
And by cloud and thunder,
his javelin breath
he installs
as part of his hobby-horse role.

He explores
my pores
my bones
my hair
my mind
till I am drenched in sweat
(or Bacchus wine)

Oh these hedonistic perversions
leak untainted
into our very souls.
Precious,
yet deleterious in the extreme.

This dissolute life
leaves me with only an insinuation of a god;
leaves but a skerrick of truth.
If only there had been
the dictatorial presence in my youth
-a 'hitler' movement of peace-

then conscience may have sought to choose
a nimbler path,
where sirens rather
would have steered
the inner eye.

Tony Woodward

All about me

the station limped to a dead stop
so I stooped to the brass bowl
now verdigris
ever smooth
my lips slurping at the
nimble spurting water stream
and cool as ice it came
flying farewells to Zurich
in girdled towels
soaking up my dripping
lips

they tease me with stiffened peaks
cream-whipped hard cartilage
as rock
building my future
with youth
with stockinged calves
it is decadence itself that decays
leaving the crisp nudity of birth
and rebirth

as sounds of snow
and egg-beaters
clatter out my death wish

Poem for Lucas

Part I

The pain suddenly beams from all Jewish ranks;
from boy to synagogue king.
Hands, which once held ivory gleam
beneath their fingernail matt sheen,
now are teeth
with godless smiles.
If Wagner had only spun his myth
with less demon-shaped threads,
the ageing uncles may have survived;
the innocent white flesh
of private boyish pianists
might have grazed even whiter loins.

We are drowned in gas;
lungs spreading like great storm clouds
before the thunderous applause.
Only here could I dream of 7th row seats.
Only here is one able to catch
the fatal blasts of the shepherd's horn.
(do not attract his attention)
(do not abide by the laws of audience)
I am the velvet carrier.
I am the silken octave.

Part II

Dancing through love and death
in an East German past,
I cradle your future children's children
in a nest of excavated ivory.
Though I should not present you thus,
while conscience presides over intellect.

Dawn is here!
With snow fretting within a withered utopian forecast.
I send you carriage and cloak.
I send you the five lines of love,
whereupon the darting ebony under your mother's wrists,
etch in black
the lark's footprints-
those final moments of the devotion lieder.
As perfect as this moment may seem,
I still fear the speed of the blacksnake's tongue.

Poem for Kathy

While sensitivity presides over intellect,
I dance through love, as each note finds the air.
And the future
cradles itself in an East Allgemeine past.
But I should not present you with this-
a nest of old polished elephant tusks.
For you!
New ivory!

And now the dawn is here-
snow fretting from memories of a withered Utopian past.
I send you carriage and cloak.
I send you five lines of love,
where,
from the softest ebony touch
beneath your mother's darting wrists,
you etch in black,
notes from an unseen score-
those final moments of the devotion lieder-
a son's love, willing itself westward
from the sullen greys of Friesburg.

As perfect as this moment may seem
under this vast sentimental sky,
I still stand in trembling awe
of the unseen trumpeter,
whose notes of gold
drift towards the sun.

Allah's Joy

One hour before the bewitching hour,
the lungs of engines
steam below the four spires;
there's too much sorrow…
    You are each pace not there.
    You are every smile not there.
Collapsed, like an oriental folded fan,
your image bound within,
protected by cheap perfect Turkish spines,
you will again unfold,
to intoxicate
to hover,
as the gulls do sail
above Hagia.

My fingernails carve at the frozen air-
ice sculptures at each step,
strewn behind me in the mists of Allah.
And so I return to golden velvet-maroon,
as if on a pink lysergic trip.
And for each gilt miniature rim,
whose detail also bids enchantment;
whose filigree is as the design of breath.
Sweet steam into the minaret night,
our breaths shall not dissolve
though our fingers shall entwine
within those crystalline sculptures scratched.

I return to a million lit memories within the mosque-
every word a smile;

every smile
your gift through Allah.
Ah! My surface is now resolute with inlay.
Should we belong?
Should we bind?
Should we die
with all of Istanbul's rose-scented veils?
In a wooden room we shun light,
time,
ennui.
Within the translucent quietude,
we swarm with love,
our kisses blessed by the bluest night,
our passion lit by the Ottoman stars.
And at the centre of this life's arid course
we swim in an oasis,
watered by the spring of our tears of joy.
And,
often floating,
are quenched by the blood of our love.

Tony Woodward

On waking again

That precise sunrise,
when the fires were lit.
What did you offer those very private gods?

Oh God! GOD!
This is the world we didn't choose.
They go, as if to say,
'Is that it?'
They come, as if to say,
'Freedom'
Or should they have said, 'Peace'?

Or should I say
'This world needs one hell of a fucker to reverse the trend,
and lead us towards a purer life of love'.
?

Desert Blue

the clouds traverse
like scorpions across a desert blue
leaving their claw prints
on god's great gibber plain

i am the god of all things
i am the god of my thongs
as worn as penitent souls

Subject to death

farinaceous
the yellow pleats in Welsh white
skin
whose pores pray for air
and once hazel hue
now china clay
hewn greenstone eyes
tomorrow-next-life-eyes set glazed

from her karst cave space
she knits needles
slice
like knives to memories
falling as smoke onto my Welsh moors
straight-edge dreams
ribboned from reality
summon newly invented words of syllabic bullshit

Greenaway winds blow
round mason-corner pose
yearning for la Scala import themes
no place for operatic sprees
they huddle instead
before the bells
anchors thrown
towards the end of life

Damaged Goods

You've lugged my heart a little too far;
the lousy poet with white flag
stuck at half-mast,
like some shallow divorce might linger aloft.
Our dissentient minds glued
to their own schools;
all feelers exterminated on outset,
axed in casual consent.

We have dialogue to spare.
We have mitigated our crimes.
We have sufficed in love
       in the vernacular,
       in death,
       infinity

'Evermore',
you had said-
a poet unleashed upon my chest.
It was then,
such hyperbole of style, when
your smile glued itself to its own teeth.
But I believed in that single device
and carved with my own tongue and saliva,
a new insignia.

The police have come, led you
away
to become more white
than angels.

The River

The river counts a billion stars
then returns to a babble.
It seizes each weathered pebble
in a Turkish embrace.
And they in turn
stroke the willowing river's cheeks,
seeking out the bank's rougher tors:
its diamonds
its sapphires
its garnets
its moonstones
its emeralds.
Then, with a glimpse of topaz hue,
it swells with ides of vice;
reflections ready to erode,
til tunnels deep
have left the boulders bare.
It is of smoky sensuality
that topaz sings tonight.
Like old resin
gathered in a wooden crease-
the uncture of love;
the search for a sea deceased.

Mirror in the Dunes

The sand shakes
Across the ridge of dunes comes the tanned man
The elephant mind
Overtures of heat rise and
Wobble the eyes
Left imagining the
Snake basket blind
And possessed
Are all the gulls full of the devil voice
Squandering gulped air
Crack open the shattered larynx
Croon-croon from skyward beak

The tanned man stands oblivious
His walk a woman's
Drenched in curves of weightlessness
Falling in leaps from the dunes
Tipped green with tea-tree fumes
And the sand rolls with each foot's gouge
Grains running upon each other
As though to smother
Settle at last

It is Easter
Last warm kiss from the sun
He descends towards the waves to rinse
Our man drifts into the sea
Sipping his salted lip
Then crucifies himself

On his browned back
On his red-hot sand

Left over in the million tiny leaves
Ragged billabong T and Velcro flies beside
Lies the perfect boy weeping
For sanity
For virginity
On the tea-tree carpet pile
Red welts of love and hate
Left like cigarette burns

Blues for Allah

Arabic spires
and diamonds adorned,
parchment transformed.
Ladders of faith left us to
the first aspirant cry.
The Imam sways at the height
of the gulls that float by.

And here, grounded,
I lay once more;
almost pulverised by the power.
A sound so prolific –
a liberated city cries.
Yet, how it taunts sweet liberty,
whose ropes about its wrists entwined
Allah's silent mile.

I prepare to slide aloft once more,
to a new diamond-studded cloud
of cuniform-quick;
of black moonless night
adrift between Allah and the upward stroke.

As the mood inspires
and minarets lance the heart,
I enquire:
'Who has sent you
to cushion my knees?
Who is that setting my heart at ease?'

Volatile Sincerity

Silhouetted against your taciturn wounds
My fingers feeling for the wet of blood
I fled the scene that day
When sophisticated knives
Knew their pattern; knew to carve
Impressions in unpretentious and honest steel
Only to be given over to vice
When we felt the cold
There in those honourable museums

I lift your blue eyelids in sleep
To see you in warrigal scenes
Unearthing witchety white-fellas along the years
Your weaponry on show

(Run and hide
My darling little brother,
For when the eagle flies
And the beak is alive with spume
The ballroom lies idle)

My Love

I have seen you intravenously,
calling on the scent of pastels
outside the window
in a light of intimate beauty,
just a hint of the secrets to follow.
Those particles of dust
caught by your eyes,
forming filigree patterns
of spiders and lies.
Your intransigence
muscles in on my love.

The Germ

I, as the germ, cast ruffled lash glances
looking for difference;
or indifference.
I am full of it:
Specious remarks that hinder my children's discernment.
Foul of breath blowing solid air,
spume, and spit,
like blowflies forging maggots upon my lips-
Woomera-laced barbs
in lexical jungles
where no-one bothers to explore.

Growling epiglottis closes for a breath;
the cords tremble
at the thought of my next idea,
the worst of which festers upstairs.
A germ inherent in sin and pain
moves from hand to mouth,
mouth to death.
(and then some)

Latent everything enters
reads the script
passes no judgement
                              sidles to the wings
                                        to the wings
to covet the audience's screams.

f words (with definite article)

the fracture bones gouged black skin and drapes
the fragments of her past in pieces arranged
the franchise of munificent gifts left
the formality we now call sleep alarmed
the frontier just beyond tomorrow
the fog of expertise in pallid hands
the forsaken sitting gutter riddled
the folklore binding her skin and spit
the fallacy mauled by the passing of clouds
the foliage parted in a child's game
the fanatic resting her arm on his
the foreigner spilling culture like milk
the fiend time in rivers of gall
the façade behind wooden paling fences
the features soft into curtain laced light
the friend of my life eating out my heart

I am to blame

Am I still the anger of your smile
scavenging for a door out,
a broken tooth,
an extraction?

Forests of joy blow in from the south,
fastidiously lifting the corner curls
on even the meanest of mouths.

Along the beach aways-
just above the spinifex line-
you bronze between the hillocks,
and the sounds burrow.

A distant osprey coasting up the southern cliffs meows.
Small waves on the outer bar
breaking into a s-mulch-shsh,
collapse harder onto the shore's
tanned boards.

Time,
on a grain of sand,
burrows too.
Tall fingers like tendrils,
clutch at DNA strands-
their tired eyes
panning for errant genes.

Yes,
I am to blame
for the cancers of our youth,
as they pick up their mallets
and smash our skulls in
while we dream of growing old.

The Mountain (for Heath)

Having ridden away into the firs,
you leave your lover's taste.
My first thought is to burst into tears.
But I soon recover from that dappled vision,
and run my hand across the front of my moleskins-
as if for some comfort.
Yes, like velvet.
Like your swollen breast,
red from my scented teeth.
So I resume an exploration under
heavy petting.
I loosen the reins where there are no reins.
I ride on freedom's quarter horse,
whose neck knows too well its prey.
And a savage gust from the frozen peaks beyond
is mauled by the teeth from my own jaws.

Yet you lay as still as ever,
under a sky
heavily predisposed so,
drinking in the mountain air, and big cats, and wolves.

So I undid your shirt,
whose tent flaps were taken up and aside
to reveal a patterned ingot.
And there
inside,
I crawled over every golden mile,
I alone knowing the signs.
Pectoral fields

of bronze,
of grain,
I reap again and again.
(It is so often, that I can hardly stand at the midnight mirror)

The moss that suffered no fear under our hooves
sprang back as we ventured deeper into the mountain.
I held your hand without a sound-
without knowing-
as if you were asleep.
And I travelled over all manner of your closed eyelids
until they shone like tiny blue-oiled domes.
Yet still you were without knowledge of your fame.

Forbes Hotel

Some are poised, ready for the fall.
Some are posed, waiting for them all.
Men can find the perfect sermon's scree.
Man can feel God's hand upon his knee.

I pushed the needle in
I pushed the knife in
I pushed the prick in
I pushed the love in

It was black beneath the well's embrace
dark black bugger kissed me in the face
Fuck you she said
then
Fuck you she sighed
I only met her once
A dash of lemonade is a dash of lemonade I almost cried
(Excuse me. Can you pour half of that out, please?)

blonde
walks
in
without
registering
the
wings,
which,
tethered
there,
unheard,

unseen,
longed
to
embrace.

abject cage

abject cage
the Doppler-effect of birdsong;
sugary but sure.
we ache for a kiss
but there,
it wavers
heavy on the mind.
and she turns to the thin air
to find he is gone.

translucent curtains
between our smiles
aching for that safety-
that pleasant satisfaction called love.

our fingers poised on hands
glance towards the veils,
which are slid ever so slightly aside.
slowly, eyes to eyes,
brimming with light and knowledge.
her happiness,
bound as ever to her peasant past,
coils about her bones,
feeds his love into her very marrow
and laughs the dream to its end.

Riding the Grey

A sunstruck bunch of strelitzias
Glowing under a balcony
The boy on his horse let free the reins
And together with dirt sounds
And breathing
They shot off
The stinging sun soon gone

A grey with flared nose
The naked thighs banging against
His horse's flanks
So that he feels their speed hit deep in his gut

Summer clouds mushrooming in a similar grey
Expand relentlessly
Then soften into rain-stuffed manes

The sun again
In all its opiate qualities lights a pink rose
Petals flash shadows on their inner flesh
While everything is stirring in the heavens

Message stick – the doors to oblivion

The light comes back on
Fear, treasured memories, nauseous no-remedy blues
Mum hovers and is lost
A life lived
So short
So kind
You come out raw screaming for air
Not sensing the danger until well into life
The reaction has been formidable upon the soul
So you ask yourself not to cast your love so readily
That which burned too long
Now hangs to desiccate in this drying gale

You can't sleep
Spirits loose yet caring pervade the mind
Until tears offer truce
And water flows towards a life of new meaning-
The constant capitalism or
The inconsistent truth-
You fret at either door

You even took on the dancer the dreamer
The arms that went out like eternal ribbons around the world
And winds and doldrums
Kept the beat
The bells sounded out
Soft and distant
As light entered the space through which you walked
Intricate harmonious and echoes of bliss

You opened the song of your heart
And sang to the end of the tunnel ahead
The insanity of a life without God
Is growing ever more feasible
The unreal becomes real
You can then open the doors to oblivion

Shackled and forced to bleed
Through the wounds of society and its morals
Guilt is superimposed by the ability not to accept
And there lies the gaping chasm-
Residue to further entangle oneself
Within the knots of unexplained offerings

Tony Woodward

The New World of Oncology

They do not suspect the
Raw eyes that were
Lipsticked by salt at 4am
Or the ribs scared to move
Frozen gauze encased
Like tundra dreams
The breath held in
As solid-night air

There are no screams
No prejudices
Not even a judicial system
In this new world

They do not suspect
The smaller ears that had
Siphoned the sounds of glitter
Those sounds of g l i t t t er

Explosions
So quiet beside the sea
And she stringing saline beads
Behind her lipstick-eyes

Pittwater

The ferry
kissing Currawong shores
almost not churning the bottom
of this
low
low
low tide-
West Head as jealous as.
For the ferry stops its northward
embrace then turns
and turns
its back on lust
for Palmy.
This very afternoon
with clinging haze
the sun blinds
across the miles of bay.
Dead seaweed sand sculptures
remind that
life has its ends-
its decay.
Even as slow as the rocks below
as that Barrenjoey lamp
erodes the dusk.

for the dead in space (after Tom Rapp)

Found those cross-road blues
they all green and sad
in eyes I choose
bleeding
like wounds in a crying storm

She stops discriminating
sky from sea
stops casting pearls
in deed
to sweep up faith's residue

When all her eyes
close
and that hand
crawls from space
to skin

No
discriminating ain't
no way to turn
when you're facing
that old solar flare

Caspian Tern

She plays upon the wind outlined
In black against the Andaman sky
Carving her arcs behind the more
Intricate patterns of the schizoid swallows
How she soars
Like an idea of Einstein's
Trapped though
In mortal coils
Her talons gradually loosen

To the left prey the dusky silhouettes
Jungle lines that recede in paler
Hues as if scalpel-cut
Will she wait for me to die of cancer
too?
I can imagine the long hospital stints
Recovering then slipping
Hoping then dying
At last

One swallow sends me crazy he
Seems larger than the rest of the summons
Huge arcs left after a spitfire flight
Those cramped chaotic spaces of
Individual trajectories

Meanwhile the Andaman girl with
Heavy le crayon khol eyes checks the points
Of each cushion and bashes
A puff of air into them.

She ensures the tops of the cushions
Have two cat's ears and a neat
Parabola of sorts between.

The railings of this jail are of raw wood
Left open to the air
Open to every thought that escapes
My eyes

I have loved so hard in the wake
Of disbelief.
I can do no more than
To argue my case with the Lord.

At Every Breath

The small knives that creep beneath
Open my veins in slow solemn promises
And viscid it doth flow toward
The dam of my own death.
There
sheltering under the great eucalypts
The flow now silently still
It waits for God's hands to cup
And carry to the altars wide.

At every breath she lifts the ruffled sheets
To show that I have not lost her yet
How to fathom the beauty at death's sweet mirror
Does she see these thoughts through
Her slightly opened eyes?
Alas
She is of another dream.

Tony Woodward

Ofuro (Into the bath)

The knuckles bled
From punches that had hit home
On his face were welts fine
As folded herringbone
He lazed sore and naked in the wooden tub
There was disbelief that the bath had been drawn
By that kimono-ed girl
With painted lips on her white encrusted rise-
The red line not following her pursed volcano peak

She had sat though
With fingers of silk
Skimming the flat flat steaming surface
The tips of his nipples sat plimsol-line raw
Where she had bitten and scratched a new map
Deeper down where the wooden walls
Had sunk the water remained burning hot
His genitals swollen
His pride drowned
Between knees bent
His yukata the only sense of light
Hung warm blue on a cold white

Why was he waiting? He was sure
She would be curled now under the kakebuton
Her black hair adrift
Onyx upon the pillows
While he watched the blood from his hands
Gradually expand in billows
Into the bath

LSD

You could not possibly be absolved yet

You still entice them to the web

You are too young a Catholic

You cast skipping stones from the shore

and watch the footprints of Jesus recede

Iceland Wind

Walked to the Iceland wind
To gaze into a sculptured sea
Stiff now from bitterness and lies
Her body in aqua deep
Sensing the hidden
Forgiving in smiles and shivers of love

It was the native stones turned bronze
All wet with mist
That I left above
The broken waves
As paper-thin tears and skin

Needing to return
To the melting summer ocean
And the joy of a spinnifex chase
We ran through the past
Avoiding the chilblained caresses

But love
Caress me now
Caress
Before the summer comes to its end
Before the melting sands stain
Your tired fears

I will conquer
And take refuge in the knowledge
That I will conquer

We are
We were
We will be
The pure lovers
The monotony of such intense love
Steels us for the rabid fusing
Lips will lock infinity in
Within the moisture of life's memories
My love Bev
Is infinite

Perchance to dream

Perchance to dream of mists
That lift
Like some organic prowl
While fingernails cling to
Perfumed parchment unduly touched
To become the manner of all hope

From the crevices of heaven
Rendered with cloudless blue
Seep memories that would choke
A world of men
And perhaps their children too

I feast upon this gilden stage
My eyes
Less fathomable for it
Sting with remorse-
The tears of rueful woe

Ah! The curl of naked shoulders
Limp with age
The mold of incessant hugs
From lovers kin and toddlers too

And oft not I come to this:

The battlefields have turned to dust
The soldiers all having chosen rust
Time's at hand and shall not flee

Nor rest upon this timeless sea

(In loneliness I came
And
In loneliness
Shall disappear)

I was born stupid

I was born stupid
with no future.
The old false dawns-
no end to 'em.
And my eyes look out
straight into crook vision-
light screaming towards
anti-substance and non-meaning.

And I sit now with white bristles
waiting for a leprechaun visit,
like the old tiny Irishman
with a pint in his eye.

Crying they are,
for the mystery.
And then
the touch of death-
desiccating down to the barnacle of form.
A slap across the hand.
A gash across the wrist.
I remonstrate.
But the sea races slowly on,
while the headless riders
learn to master their runaway steeds.

I hang now,
strung from my own taught forearms-
stretching creatively for breath.
My spirit leaves,

and leaves,
and leaves.
And all sin is buried
with the end of my voice.

LaVergne, TN USA
02 February 2011
214843LV00001B/14/P